CHANGE IN MANUFACTURING

THE ONE CONSTANT

A life's experience and what I've learned

Bedford "Buff" Bruno

November 2017

INTRODUCTION

As I near 65 and enter my "first retirement" phase, it seems like a good time to reflect on learnings and create some structure that summarizes how my approach has evolved in managing significant change situations. Looking back on my career, change seems to be the one constant. My uniqueness centers around the number of different situations that I have entered with the primary responsibility of leading significant change because of some external shock or due to expectations of step change improvements quickly. I managed my first plant in 1987 and have been in manufacturing leadership roles ever since. The bookend experiences of my career are from taking over a small plant (80 colleagues) that had to close within a year in 1987; to acquiring a plant in Montreal, Canada with 500 colleagues and state of the art technology and moving it to Dover, DE while closing and selling the Canadian facility in 2017. In between those 2 experiences are others that will be discussed in this book. My intent is to describe the experiences, challenges and results; and develop a framework than can be useful to others as they engage in large scale change situations. My hope is that this work is useful to others and that it will enable me to reach out and be a resource in the next phase of my career and life.

This book is organized in a way that provides the reader with some background of my early years and how change was engrained in my thinking, as well as, a description of the significant change leadership experiences of my career. After that background review, I develop a methodology for leading and managing significant change situations. It is intended to give leaders a guide to help them negotiate the landscape and be a positive force for change. Although I've included some illustrations to help the reader conceptualize the process, it is not intended to be a checklist but more of a process to use starting from Day 1 out to stability and sustainment. I end the book with a closing note and some final reflections.

THE CHAPTERS

1. Background
    a. The Early Years and the Army (1975-1979)
    b. The First Plant Manager Roles – Close and Significant Downsize (1987-1991)
    c. Automotive – Starting Up Plants Around the World (1996-2000)
    d. Endgame – Major Plant Consolidation and Closure (2013-2017)
2. Assessment Phase
3. Planning Phase
4. Implementation Phase
5. Continuous Improvement and Renewal
6. Supporting Processes and Systems
7. Closing Note

1. BACKGROUND

The Early Years and the Army

My father was in the Army for 36 years. He retired a Full Colonel after progressing through all the ranks starting with Private. That made me a "military brat" as we were referred to in the Army and other branches of military service. It meant that we moved from station to station with our parents throughout our formative years. I lived in 10 different places to include Japan by the time I got out of high school. Change for me was a way of life as every couple of years everything in my world would be different and I would have to figure out how to adapt. I learned pretty early that sports was a great way of integrating into any new environment and making new friends. So that was my process — when we got to a new location, find a basketball court and with that you will get new friends. I also joined every team that I could so I was engaged in team sports throughout the year. For me adapting to change was about proactively engaging the new world in a way that was fun and challenging. It's a mindset and one that I would use continually to learn, grow and develop.

After I graduated from college I joined the Army like my father and learned the Army way of doing things. From basic training and throughout my 4 years of active duty, I was taught to do my job at every stage of my development. In basic training you are the lowest of the low and the drill instructors build you up after breaking you down and getting rid of all your "bad habits". Once you learn the fundamentals, you start to develop and build your own uniqueness and maximize your contribution to whatever team you are a part of. The military is about learning and being open to others in the process. Take yourself out of it and get the most of new situations; and then you can extend yourself to the maximum. 6 weeks of basic training and then another 9 months of Engineering Officer basic training would prepare me to join a unit and start to contribute to the "good of the corps and the service"!!

I joined the 13th Engineering Battalion of the 7th Infantry Division based at Fort Ord, CA. The Division was newly formed so I was one of the first officers to join our unit as we were building it up to full strength. The primary role for a new 2nd Lieutenant in an Engineering Battalion was a Platoon Leader. I was the first officer to move into that role with my Platoon. Our mission was to support an infantry battalion and combat operations. Since it was a new platoon, my focus was on getting our operational readiness up to the standards that had been established. As the Army does, those standards were clearly defined in a manual -- so the focus was individual training, squad level training and then, finally, platoon level training. I had 1 Platoon Sergeant and 4 Squad Leaders that were senior non-commissioned officers and knew their job well. My job was to let them do their job and, then, adding value where I could. I also had to learn the job and strengthen my leadership skills. The military focuses on training to a high level of competence (being all that you can be) and maintaining high levels of discipline in the process.

Subsequent to my Platoon Leader role, I became the Headquarters Company Executive Officer and then the Commanding Officer to round out my 4 years of experience on active duty. Within the Headquarters Company were all of the support units for the battalion — I.e. Mess Hall, Maintenance, Planning Sections. But the company also had all of the heavy construction equipment (Graders, Bulldozers) that were necessary to do the road and airfield construction projects. Although my role with the Headquarters Company was a heavy dose of administration, the construction leadership part provided for a lot of engagement with the Air Force and other units while executing critical missions.

The Army was the best training ground that I could have hoped for in getting ready for manufacturing leadership roles. Learn your job, know your job and do your job — these were the fundamentals of every role that I have taken on since. The importance of leadership is stressed at every level — it's not "in addition to" but fundamental to every role or job that you do. It centered around people and ensuring that they have the skills that they need and that they are performing within their team in a way that is truly value added with no negative, disruptive energy!!

Beyond that, you have to be a model for what leadership looks like and you have to be value added to whatever organization you are a part of, or task that you take on. It was tough to leave the Army as it was all that I knew, but something was pulling me forward. So, I took the leap, but I couldn't have had a better learning experience.

First Plant Manager Roles – Close and Significant Downsize

I was in the Army from 1975-1979 and it would take until 1987 for me to get my next significant leadership role. Between the Army and that time I was "learning the civilian world" starting as an individual contributing Project Engineer and working my way up to leadership roles on the technical side of Plant Operations. In 1987 I left Frito Lay as a Technical Manager at their plant outside of Detroit, MI to take on my first Plant Manager role in South Carolina. The plant was a non-woven facility that made resin bonded rolls of material that were converted by customers into dryer softener sheets. The plant was the initial operation started by an entrepreneur and had older technology. Upon arrival I was given the mission to turn things around in 6 months or make plans to close the operation and move the business to a newer plant and technology just down the road. My first order of business was to communicate the situation to the plant colleagues and ask for their support. Then, together with the leadership team, we developed our plan and managing process to turn things around. At the end of the day, we were able to make significant improvements but not sufficient to make the operation viable for the future. In the process we had developed a tight knit, family orientation that served us well to the very end. We closed the plant within a year of me taking the role and were able to place everyone in jobs within the community. I deemed it a success as we met the needs of the business and the people and it was an extremely fulfilling experience.

As luck would have it, just as I was completing my first Plant Manager assignment, the Plant Manager of our largest plant was moving on and I was given that position. Going from a plant of 80 that was closing to one of 180 with 7 day a week production was a big jump in scope for me, but I was pumped and ready for the challenge!! A couple of months into the role, we were notified by one of our largest customers that they were moving their business to another supplier. For us that meant a 40% reduction in production volume and going from a 7-day to 4-day operation. Instead of growing the plant and business, I was back in the survival game with a new mission of downsizing the plant to be able to sustain its viability for the future.

This was a relatively new plant that had been developed with a very traditional organization and a lot of hierarchy — 6 levels from shop floor operator to Plant Manager. It was a new leadership team for me, and I was coming to the team with the baggage of just closing the plant down the road, but I used the same process of communication and openness. The previous plant manager was more private and traditional in his leadership style. He didn't engage all levels of the organization but mainly worked through his leadership team. So right out of the gates, I increased my communication and engagement to all levels and functions of the organization. I was fortunate to have a boss who was very knowledgeable on some of the "leading edge" organizational approaches to manufacturing. He gave me a couple of consultants to contact as I worked to develop our approach. The challenge was to size the plant organization in line with the current production demands, but with the flexibility to adapt quickly to increases in demand. I was leading and learning again trying to develop myself as a thought leader relative to a new organizational design.

We were able to reduce the organization by 1/3 initially which meant a layoff of about 60 folks. But we did this in a way that moved us into a "self-managing" team organization and 3 levels of hierarchy from Plant Manager to shop floor operator. This was done through a series of Leadership Workshops where all levels of leaders learned a common language and framework to operate by. There were no supervisors or watchers or checkers — everyone had a value added role to the mission and worked together to help others so that the plant could be successful. This organization was "scalable" and when volume moved back to a 7-day operation, the plant organizational size remained relatively stable. This significantly improved the plant cost position and secured the future for the plant. The plant eventually leveled off at just over 100 colleagues with increases in volume compared to the initial 180 colleagues when I assumed the Plant Manager role.

I moved on from this role into the next level of leadership as a Director of Manufacturing. This involved more of steady state operations and continuous improvement situations. Clearly my first 4 years in my first 2 Plant Manager roles provided the experiences around change management that would serve me well in the future.

Automotive – Starting Up Plants Around the World

The next significant change experience came as I moved into the automotive world as a Plant Manager for an operation that was 6 months removed from its initial start-up. This was a privately held French company that supplied bumpers and fuel tanks directly to the automaker's production lines. Over a 5 year period I would lead 2 plant start-ups (1 in South Carolina and another in England) and be the overall Project Lead for a 3rd in Mexico. Each situation was different and required its own unique approach. My learnings from this period were significant from an organizational and cultural perspective. This represented the period from 1995 to 2000.

In the first situation in South Carolina, I arrived late in the start-up and was playing catch-up for the first 6 months. The initial start-up team was still running the show and there had been a limited transfer of knowledge. My job was to grab hold of the current issues and ensure we were addressing them in a timely manner, and then to get the right organization in place to sustain and improve the operation. I arrived in crisis and within 6 months we had moved to stability; then the task was to get to an improved level of performance and profitability. Simultaneously with the above I had to give our customers confidence that we would be able to meet their needs. I had to project both internally and externally that confidence and it had to be based on real and significant progress.

After a year of intensive activity in South Carolina, there was a need to start up a plant in England just north of Birmingham. Because of my experience in South Carolina, I was asked to take on that leadership role both from an overall project perspective and the ongoing operation of the plant. I jumped into that role immediately while the family completed the school year in South Carolina. I was anxious to ensure we were taking the proper actions to get resources in place early and have the critical mass in place before the production start. I was fortunate to have 2 gentleman who were extremely capable of handling the technical and engineering side of the project. One was our Project Manager from Paris and the other our Engineering Manager in the UK. This enabled me to focus on the organizational and recruitment aspects of the project. I was relentless in my recruiting to ensure we got the best folks for the key roles and that they joined us well in advance of the production start.

Once the team was in place it was just a matter of aligning around organizational roles and expectations and ensuring everything was linked to the Project Plan. My role once the organization was in place was about direction, guidance and collaboration. Our start-up was considered a model for the company as we exceeded all expectations and hosted visitors from around the world. I incorporated my learnings from my early plant leadership roles and we implemented self-managing work teams from the start. Our new colleagues took to the new approach and it created an energy level that was the hallmark of the plant. We had open office areas and, with the number of different cultures and languages, you could always hear a "buzz" reflecting the energy and excitement!!

The 3rd situation was for a plant that was in the project phase in Mexico. GM was the primary customer and they were very unhappy with the progress and communication to date. The need for my role was basically to ensure that the project plan was in place and progression was in line with the expected timing from the customer. And then it was about communication to the customer in a way that they had an increased confidence level in our company and the project. The key learnings in this situation were mainly cultural ones. The customer was out of Detroit with expectations clearly out of the American automotive playbook — do it as I say when I say. The technology development was done in Lyon, France with a very flexible process that at times would get out of alignment with the customer. And, finally, the plant was in Saltillo, MX in a culture that was laid back and somewhat corrupt. Recognizing the complexity of the project and the interaction of the cultures, I found it necessary to be in Mexico almost every week. In every meeting we had the 3 different cultures represented — some spoke 1 language (like me); some 2 and a very few understood all 3 languages. It took significantly more time understanding and aligning within the project team, and it was critical for me to be the documenter and communicator of our decisions and actions. My role focused on the blocking and tackling of the project to ensure that we stayed the course and that the customer was fully integrated into our plans. As that project entered start-up and the French company decided to halt its expansion in the US, I looked for other opportunities and moved on.

For the next 13 years I continued to play the primary leadership role in a number of different manufacturing situations. I left automotive and took on a plant manager role in a small specialty chemical operation that was highly profitable. This was for a 5-year period that included a union contract negotiation. The expectation was to significantly increase capacity and reduce overhead. Both were achieved through efficiency gains and headcount reductions. I then took on the leadership role for a start-up wet wipes business that was part of a privately held absorbent products company. The operation was manual and labor intensive. The expectations were to automate and bring internal the production of the primary raw materials. Most of this was achieved prior to moving on to the next opportunity. In 2006 I joined Playtex Products (they were eventually bought by Energizer) and started as Director of their Ohio operations. This was a small operation (<200) as we consolidated everything into one site and closed the other in a 2-year period. Next, I moved to Dover to take on a business unit lean leadership role before assuming overall leadership for the Fem Care Operations in 2010.

Endgame – Major Plant Consolidation and Closure

The next significant change leadership role for me came about in 2013 and continued until my recent retirement. I was with Energizer when it started and then the company split in two with my operations being part of a new company called Edgewell Personal Care. It is a company with some leading brand names — Schick, Banana Boat, Hawaiian Tropic, Wet Ones, Diaper Genie and Playtex. I started in the company leading the Wet Ones, Playtex Gloves and Diaper Genie operations and then moved to the Fem Care brands — Gentle Glide and Sport tampons. In 2013 we jumped into the mix of companies considering acquiring the J&J North American Fem Pro business (Carefree Liners, Stayfree Pads, and OB tampons). I was heavily involved in the early due diligence work. We ended up acquiring the business at the end of 2013 and I was given the operational lead for the acquired brands as we considered the consolidation of all the production in Dover, DE. After extensive analysis the project was approved in June of 2014. We would move all manufacturing operations from Montreal to Dover, DE and close the Montreal plant. The Montreal plant employed over 500 colleagues with 500,000 SF of manufacturing space — it was identical in # of colleagues and size to the Dover plant. At the end of the project 2 significantly underutilized plants would be consolidated in Dover with its population growing to 700 colleagues and the manufacturing space increasing slightly to 550,000 square feet.

I assumed leadership for the consolidation project and continued to lead all of the Fem Care operations in the interim (both the Dover and the Montreal operations). The initial plans called for the consolidation to be completed by May of 2017 based on a start of July of 2014. This was considered a very aggressive plan from the start as we were pushed by senior leadership and consultants to continually improve our estimates. We completed the project with all production lines moved and in commercial production in August of 2017 — an unbelievable task given the complexity of the production and process equipment that we were moving. My role was straightforward — get the Montreal and the Dover organizations to work together in such a way that 1/ The project was completed on-time; 2/ There were no significant customer outage issues; and 3/ The savings specified in the project were delivered.

In simple terms the key components of the project were: 1/ Disconnect, move and reconnect all operations in Dover and transfer all information necessary to operate them; 2/ Continue to operate the Montreal plan in the interim in a stable way with no deterioration of results; and 3/ Build the organization and capability in Dover necessary to operate, maintain and sustain all production requirements. My focus was on 2 and 3 — #1 was led by very capable technical professionals that were experienced, knew the job, and were driven to get it done.

My focus in Montreal was proactively supporting that team and ensuring they were actively involved in the project every step of the way, and that we cared about their future and would support them through severance and other ways of helping in their transition. I initiated a "leadership team" process where every 2 months we had coordination meetings in Montreal with all key leaders from all functions attending. This included the full Montreal leadership team as well. We wanted to be transparent and ensure that all of our decisions were based on sound rationale and were well supported by the entire team. Our Senior VP, who was on the company's top leadership team, attended one of our meetings and said to me "I'm shocked at the level of engagement of the total team — no hidden agendas or negative behaviors with everyone on one team looking out for the best interests of the company and the project!!" That was my primary job and I knew how important it was to the success of the project.

My other key involvement area was to ensure that the receiving organization in Dover was in place early to ensure the necessary capability for a successful start-up. All of my experience with the automotive start-ups taught me well here. I was driven to incorporate it into this project! It was quite a ride, building a world class organization next to our existing one while trying to upgrade it as well. We ended up generally delivering the project to expectation level, and this was the culmination of my experience through the years — quite an ending to quite a ride!!!

At this point, a high-level summary of my learnings and key principles would be:

- Create that "Sense of Urgency" and be the model of the "Right Behaviors" from Day 1.
- Make sure the Organization and People are right for the situation at hand.
- Initiate rigorous planning and managing processes throughout.
- Create a culture of accountability, collaboration, action and results.
- Be relentless in executing all of the above.

2. ASSESSMENT PHASE

When you enter into a role that demands significant change in a short timeframe, your "Day 1" actions are critical to setting the stage for your leadership. My experience is that your demeanor is important to start to align the key leaders and the entire organization with your leadership approach. Learning and understanding ought to be the hallmark of your entry. You are starting to define the current situation in your mind and then test your thinking and ideas with the people in the organization. Always communicate with respect and seek to build trust at every step. To do that you must be "trust worthy" by being honest and forthright. In Day 1 you want to initiate the Assessment Phase. You don't have to be formal about it but you want to have a process to gather relevant data and information.

Some things to organize would be: 1/ One to one's with the leadership team and other key stakeholders; 2/ Slice (cross functional and multilevel) meetings throughout the organization - one with each shift of shop floor folks and with office staff; 3/ Performance Metrics reviews with the primary teams in the operation; and 4/ General Gemba (a lean term) walks in the plant asking questions and seeking feedback. These things should be done in the first week or so – it is important that people feel your presence and a sense of urgency.

The one to one's should be open ended questions as you are casting a wide net and want to fully understand the situation. Some questions might be "What do you believe are the primary issues facing this operation?" And "How do you see your role in addressing these issues?" As you get deeper into the one to ones and start to see primary issues emerging, your questions should be more specific around root causes and thoughts for corrective actions. All the time you are listening intently and taking notes. At the end of the one to ones you may ask "What questions do you have for me?" -- this is a way of understanding some more personal concerns that people may have.

The slice meetings can be structured similarly, but you'll want to probe everyone so you can feel there is consensus around the issues and concerns. In the group settings, it is an opportunity for you to build trust and confidence in your leadership ability to get things done. These meetings will also provide you with insights on possible disconnects between the shop floor shifts and the office folks.

For the metrics review meetings, I like to keep it to the key leaders in the plant – these would be the folks with the primary accountability in the key metric areas. I also like to involve those outside of the leadership team that are critical to the success of the operations. Key Performance Metric Areas usually include: Safety, Quality, Customer Service, New Product Development, Working

Capital and Cost. As I set the expectation for these meetings and what format I'm looking for, I try to create focus for the team. In Lean, the A3 process outlines the best approach. The A3 is a 11x17 sheet of paper that incorporates all aspects of the PDCA (Plan, Do, Check, Act) process. It incorporates information that answers the following questions: 1/ What are the key metrics that determine success in your performance area? 2/ What are your goals or the expected level of performance in these metrics? 3/ What is your current performance and recent trends relative to the metrics? 4/ What are the gaps and reasons (root causes) for not meeting the goals? 5/ What actions are necessary to close the gap and meet or exceed the goals? And 6/ Based on the action timing, what is the trajectory of improvement expected?

The best A3s are visual with graphs and pareto charts communicating the information in a way that the entire process is easily understood. Like the military's 1 page operations order, the A3 should be easily understood and give everyone confidence that you have a handle on the situation. If you can't boil it down on an A3 that is understood at a glance, then you don't fully understand the situation and you need to dig deeper.

As you gather the information outlined above, you will also be assessing the organization – where are the strengths and the weaknesses? How effective is the current organization at delivering the results? How can I align my strongest players with the most important metrics areas? How do I address organizational and individual weaknesses – identify high performance talent and promote? It is at this point that things start coming together – the "What" of the issues and concerns, and the "How" of the individual and organizational capability.

Concurrent with the work of the Assessment Phase, it is important to establish a "Lean" management process immediately. This ensures that the operations key metrics are reviewed at each level relative to performance to targets and proper actions are taken as issues emerge. The intent is when you are "out of tolerance" actions are taken immediately to get you back in, or the issue is escalated quickly to a higher level for additional resources. These managing processes are: 1/ By the hour; 2/ By the shift; 3/ By the Day; 4/ By the Week; and 5/ By the Month. This makes the organization like a "guided missile" always honing in on its objective while making continuous corrections along the way. There may be good management processes in place, but very seldom is there the level of connection that is necessary to be efficient and effective in managing the operations -- you want this process "machine like"!! This delivers the "cadence" necessary to operate effectively.

This should take you to 30 days in the job and put you in a position to develop the comprehensive plans that ensure the results that are needed are achieved. The next chapter will move into that area.

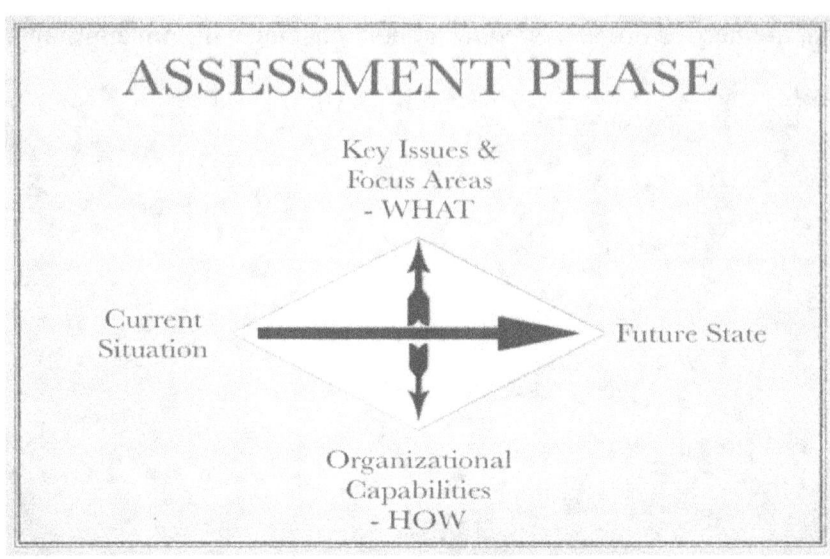

The A3 Report

Background	Future State & Countermeasures
- Why do we need to work on this? - Context - Importance	- Actions being taken to address the issue (what, who, when) - Quick fixes (Containment actions) - To Be process map
Current State	**Impact**
- Problem statement/definition - As Is process map - Scale of the problem (data)	- Results achieved - Trend graph (before/after)
Objective	**Follow-up**
- Target level of performance - Desired outcome	- Actions still required (what, who, when) - Learning points to share
Root Cause Analysis	
- Fishbone diagram - 5 Whys - Data (Pareto, Scatter diagram)	

3. **PLANNING PHASE**

While the Assessment Phase creates understanding and starts to align the organization around the key issues, the Planning Phase puts in place the rigor necessary to move the operations forward in a systemic way. It should have a standardized format throughout the operations with defined teams and leaders. The plan should be linked to individual KPIs (Key Performance Indicators) so that there is no disconnect and everyone is "singing from the same hymnal"!! In every operation there is a functional organizational chart which defines the hierarchy with roles and responsibilities – this is a picture of the way work gets done in the various functions. But when you consider step change improvement, it always happens along the material flow or value stream. In a manufacturing process, raw materials come in and are tested and converted each step of the way. Each step checks the last step and adds some value and then moves it to the next step. The work done along the value stream is cross functional, so the planning process to improve things must have all the functions involved. This will represent a different organization which operates concurrently with the functional organization. One gets the work done today, the other works to significantly improve the work and results tomorrow.

The start of the planning process is always in developing the high level "Hoshin" (a lean term). The Hoshin sets the goals of the operation and starts to organize the plan in cascading fashion. A typical Hoshin would have a cover sheet that shows the high-level key metrics in each performance area with the goal and actual performance. Next would be a Strategy sheet that shows the key strategies pursued to drive the key metrics in the right direction – it also would highlight the key leader for each strategy. The next sheet would show the focus areas for each strategy and also highlight a leader for each focus area. The Hoshin is generally high level and tracked by month using a color-coded process for progress (Green-on track, Yellow-at risk and Red-off track).

While the Hoshin Plan is high level, it starts to align and organize around the key activities -- both strategies and focus areas. It also should highlight the key leaders in the operations that are driving the change. For each focus area there should be a different process – much more detail and root cause oriented. The A3 process should be the guide for the work within the focus groups. Each focus group should have their A3 and it should be updated weekly to show progress in terms of activity and results. The Strategy Leaders should be actively engaged with their Focus area teams so that they can represent the progress in the overall monthly Hoshin review. The Focus teams should involve all key individuals and functions necessary to plan and implement improvements in that area. Even though the work is done in the functions, close coordination ensures that it is efficient and effective. The focus teams look at "optimizing" the work in order to deliver the needed results.

While the Hoshin monthly and Focus area weekly processes drive the step change improvements, the daily process keeps the ship moving to the right cadence. The Daily process is about exception management and issue resolution. It is focused along the Value Stream (or manufacturing flow) and starts with an hourly review by production line. The review focuses on the process performance and looks at quality and the production rate for that hour – it is either OK or has issues that need to be addressed. Any breakdowns or stoppages are addressed immediately, but the hourly check is a look at the overall performance for the previous hour. A shift has a kick-off meeting at the beginning of the shift where they review the issues and priorities for the day and then the "by the hour" checks guide the resource allocation during the shift. Once a day in each production area, there is a "tier meeting" that looks at the previous days performance to highlight issues and opportunities and guide the resource allocation effort – this is mandatory attendance for all local functional leaders. If an issue is significant and needs additional resources or raised awareness to higher levels, it is brought up at the next level tier meeting. An example of this system in a plant might be 3 tier meetings each day – in the production area, in the primary Value Streams, and finally a Plant level one. They might be scheduled at 8:30am, 9am and 9:30am each day. This routine provides the structure to the operations necessary to deliver the results daily.

Both of these processes are part of a "Lean" methodology. The Tier system is about delivery as efficiently as possible the results needed today, while the Hoshin planning process is about improving performance tomorrow to the trajectory that is needed to support the business. Leaders play a significant role in both processes. Once they are imbedded within an operation, improvement becomes systemic and efficiency and effectiveness are the norm. The intent is always to allocate resources in the optimal way to drive the performance in the direction needed to support the business and the larger operation.

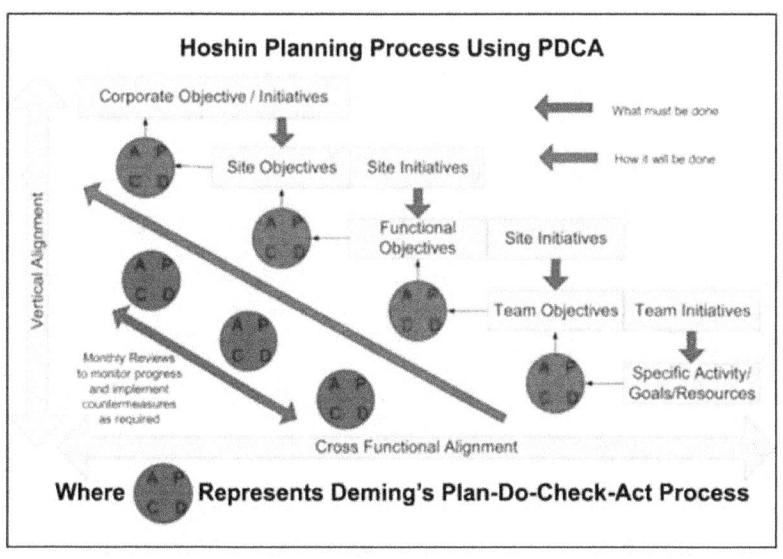

4. IMPLEMENTATION PHASE

In Implementation everything is in place to execute the plan. From a wholistic perspective it goes beyond just the plan documents and meetings. You have to consider all aspects.

From an **Operations** view you have to ensure that: 1/ The operation of the Value Stream (manufacturing flow) is fully integrated with all functions part of the teams and collaboration at a high level; 2/ Accountability should be placed at the right level with individuals and teams given the freedom to make decisions creating more agility; and 3/ OEE (Operating Equipment Efficiency) should be a part of the manufacturing DNA as teams are driving continuous improvement and seeking perfection.

From a **Human Resources** view you have to ensure that plans and objectives are reflected in the individual performance management system. Individuals should sign up for a few step change objectives each year and these should be aligned with the overall Hoshin. This thinking should extend to all colleagues and not just for the salary folks. Everyone should be given a challenging role and the freedom to make a significant difference. Recruitment and hiring should be focused on current skill gaps and future needs to include the softer skills that a critical in being value added to any organization. The culture should be defined with values and principles established and communicated on a recurring basis. It should be ever evolving to sustain a vibrant and exciting workplace.

These would incorporate the timeless values of respect for others, integrity, collaboration, accountability and agility; but will include others that are unique to each organization.

From a **Planning and Managing** view all of the documentation and meetings have to be systemically ingrained in the organization. Everyone needs to take accountability for their role and participate and be proactive in these processes. Documents should be visual (charts, tables and graphs) and simple. The principle of "at a glance" and being able to understand what is going on is critical. If primaries are unable to attend meetings, then there is a secondary. Meetings always have 100% representation from the various functions and entities. It's all about execution. If you think about all of the highly successful football programs and you listen to their coaches – practices are scripted with a focus on execution and perfection. That is what we are doing here!!

From a **Site** view we want all attention out where the action is happening. The Lean term is "Gemba" which is Japanese for "where the work is". In the manufacturing world the "Gemba" is on the shop floor where we are making product!! The focus should be always "go and see" what's happening. Tier meetings and Leadership/Functional meetings should be out where the action is. The expectation should always be perfection in how we operate our "value adding processes"! Not only is the attention from the entire organization out at "Gemba" but also the 5S methodologies and the visual management is such that you can always see what's going on. Just by looking at a production line you can tell -- 1/ Is it operating in the Green? 2/ Are there issues currently? 3/ What has been the performance in the last hour – shift – day – week? And 4/ Who are the owners of the process? 5S is the core process that sets the Lean mindset. It stands for Sort, Set, Shine, Standardize and Sustain. So, when you use 5S on a machine or process area, you use this process to start to get things in order. Sort is about only having what you need to operate the line; Set is about putting what you need at the right spot; Shine is about maintaining a high level of cleanliness throughout; Standardize is about ensuring everyone does things the same way; and Sustain is about setting an expectation of Continuous Improvement but always doing it in a Standardized way. 5S should not be just a shop floor thing but it's principles should be reflected throughout the organization.

In Implementation the Functional and Project Organizations are supplemented with other systemic processes that help tie things together. The following chart summarizes what has been discussed in this chapter. They must be fully integrated with the other plans discussed earlier.

IMPLEMENTATION PHASE

Operations
- Fully integrated at the VS.
- Accountability at the right level.
- OEE thinking - expectation of perfection.

Managing
- Monthly Hoshin meetings.
- Weekly Focus Group meetings.
- Daily Tier meetings.
- Weekly Leadership meetings

HR
- Linkage to Performance Mgmt.
- Recruitment/Hiring linkage.
- Values based interactions.

Planning
- Hoshin / A3 formats.
- Visual communication.
- Rigorous documentation.
- Clear Accountability

Site
- Gemba Walks for all levels.
- Visual communications.
- 5S to the max.

5. **CONTINUOUS IMPROVEMENT AND RENEWAL**

In managing significant change, you are hitting the ground running. You have a process, but you are really focused on the first 90 days. By that time, you've completed your assessment and planning processes; and are in implementation. This will get you step change improvement and a trajectory that meets your short-term time horizon needs. Beyond that, you want to make sure that the longer-term framework is being developed and that planning process is in place.

This is an exercise for the leadership team with input from other key stakeholders. The process starts with clearly understanding your direction 3 to 5 years out. There are many variations on how to do this, but I use a simple and straightforward one. It starts with the Purpose of the unit and organization which is the "Why do we exist?". I like organizing my Purpose statements more holistically using the following framework: 1/ TO: do what? 2/ IN A WAY THAT: gets at how and organization. And 3/ SO THAT: starts to frame the why. A simple example of the manufacturing organization's purpose may be:

To: Safely and Cost effectively manufacture and deliver finished products;

In a way that: Meets the needs of all consumers, customers and stakeholders;

So that: The brand, company and society are benefited and the plant has long term viability.

The Vision is an aspirational statement that describes the situation at some point (5 years?) in the future. It incorporates results and whatever else that you feel is important. A good process for this is the "affinity" one. Let people do a quiet brainstorm and then have them put sticky notes on a wall with each thought, and then quietly start organizing them into themes. Once you have the themes, you can prioritize them and craft the Vision. Once it is developed, step back and compare it with the Current State Landscape and identify the major gaps. The Mission flows from the gaps and clarifies the "Initial Thrust" that will get you down the road to the Vision.

With initial Direction set, the plans need to be developed that will change the current trajectory and meet the Future State requirements. The annual Hoshin planning framework is a good structure to use, but instead of using an annual timeframe you are out 3-5 years. Organizations use different long-term timeframes -- my last company used a 3-year timeframe. One process to use is to start with the Annual Hoshin and identify gaps with the Direction just established. Objectives will be different and more aggressive, there may be some strategies missing. In general, the annual Hoshin plan should incorporate the Mission and elements of capability needed to ensure Future State can be achieved; while the Strategic

Plan Direction will incorporate more capability building elements to enable a sustained long-term push.

Once the Plans are set, the organization necessary to execute those plans needs to be established. This involves the development of the formal organizational structure. What functions and their purpose? What roles within the functions? How to ensure all roles are value added and self-management is an expectation? How to build in a network and expectation of cross functional alignment around critical issues? Once the formal organizational structure is in place, processes and systems must be established that support the effective functioning of the organization. Examples of supporting processes are: 1/ Leadership team meetings (both Top and Functional); 2/ Annual planning and managing processes; 3/ Daily operations tier managing; and 4/ Functional excellence managing process. Examples of supporting systems are: 1/ Individual performance management; 2/ Financial Management; 3/ Quality management; 4/ Health, Safety, and Environmental management. These processes and systems ensure organizational alignment in the most effective and efficient way. The intent is to not waste people's time but to be value added to the more formal organizational structure.

Once the organization is set, then you are at the Renewal and Continuous Improvement stage. This normally involves quarterly / annual review and updates. This is where you step back from a big picture perspective to see what "levers" should be pulled. How can we be "bold" in our actions to accelerate our movement to the Future State? Organization is a lever that can have a major impact – both negative or positive. In general, you want to develop and align your strengths against the main issues and gaps. But you have to be careful not to "deplete" your organization in other areas that may cause results to deteriorate! Pictured next I have an illustration of a Strategic and Organizational Planning process for your reference.

STRATEGIC AND ORGANIZATIONAL PLANNING

DIRECTION	PLANNING	ORGANIZATION	RENEWAL
• Purpose (Why?) • Vision (What?) • Mission (How?) • Landscape/ Gaps	• Hoshin • Objectives/ Strategies • Focus Areas/ Milestones	• Structure/ Processes/Systems • Self-Management • Cross Functional Alignment	• Standardized Annual Planning • Systemize Planning Templates • Creative/Flexible Organizational Planning

6. SUPPORTING PROCESSES AND SYSTEMS

In order to support the Strategic direction and planning process, certain constraints have to be assessed early on to ensure full capability exists to deliver the results. These include the Organizational, Manufacturing Capacity, and Financial assessments. Some key questions include: 1/ Do we have the Organizational skills and capability to deliver the Future State? How do we "Stack the Deck" to power our way to the FS? 2/ Do we have sufficient manufacturing/production capacity? If not, where do we add and when? 3/ Is our cost structure in line with the Future State? If not, what does it need to look like and what are the implications?

These are key questions that take a significant amount of time to address. That is why they must be identified early on and action put in place to ensure proper capability exists.

Having already established the organizational plan, you will want to identify the critical resources needed to give you the push to get over the hump. This might be a few key people to add to the organization that can be the "drivers" of the change that is needed. Even though this is incremental staffing – the investment will pay for itself many times over!!

In the area of manufacturing capacity, you want to position your operations to cost effectively be able to produce what is needed. Anytime you are running 7 days 24 hours a day, it adds an incremental cost. You have to determine the optimal operating frame for your plant and business and, based on the future demand requirements, develop your capacity expansion plans. Some equipment is designed to run 7 days, and some need the downtime on the weekends so a 5-day frame makes more sense. You have to not only look at the equipment but also the organizational implications. A 7-day operation will involve more support infrastructure and costs. All this needs to be considered and built into your capacity plans both short and long term.

In the area of financial capacity, you have to "solve" the equation to determine what your costs have to be to meet the needs of the business. And then, back into the numbers. This has implications for operating production rates, efficiencies and scrap, as well as, variable and fixed overhead rates. Once you "solve the equation", then it's a matter of identifying the levers to pull and where to allocate the resources. In the overhead areas, this may mean bold decisions. You may have to take a big chunk of costs out and need to choose where to do it – what's the best use of contract resources? Once you know your gaps, it's a matter of getting them in line. But you have to make hard choices and live with them.

These are a few of the key areas to consider. Based on your business and operations there may be more – it's up to you to define them and then plan accordingly.

7. **CLOSING NOTE**

While things were fresh in my mind, I wanted to get them down into a framework and structure. My career encompassed 4 years in the Army active duty (and 12 years in the Army reserve) and 38 years in manufacturing leadership positions, of which 30 involved plant or higher leadership roles. For me, it was an opportunity to make a significant difference in the plant and business, and in the lives of people that I worked with every day. I had the pleasure of working with great folks and was fortunate enough to have mentors along the way that helped me through difficult periods and challenged me to be better. I've been married now for 43 years to a partner that was always there for me with unconditional love and support. I would not be who I am today without her and my family being there every step of the way. The major themes for me are pretty simple: 1/ Be open and seek to understand before being understood; 2/ Engage throughout the organization to enhance understanding and gain alignment; 3/ Always be positive and respectful; 4/ Drive for excellence and ensure broad accountability; and 5/ Come to work every day to make a difference.

In "The Four Agreements" (A Toltec Wisdom Book), a practical guide to personal freedom is outlined. I believe this supports my major themes above and will enable you to fulfill your potential. The Four Agreements are: 1/ Be impeccable with your word; 2/ Don't take anything personal; 3/ Don't make assumptions; and 4/ Always do your best. I like the first agreement the most. Every time you open your mouth, you make some impact in the world – make it good 100% of the time. I think if everyone followed that our world would be a better place!

www.ingramcontent.com/pod-product-compliance
Lightning Source LLC
Chambersburg PA
CBHW050030230526
45470CB00003B/1213